THE CHP BOOK OF
FAMOUS LIVES

Written By: BOB GOODWIN
                       DYMPNA HAYES

Editors: DYMPNA HAYES
                       TERI KELLY

Art Director: RICK ROWDEN

Illustrators: LORI DOWNEY
                       DENIS GAGNE
                       ROBERT JOHANNSEN
                       DALLYN LYNDE
                       KEVIN PUDSEY
                       KAREN REITHOFER
                       RICK ROWDEN
                       VICKIE ROWDEN
                       TIM ZELTNER

DURKIN HAYES PUBLISHING LTD.
3312 Mainway, Burlington, Ontario L7M 1A7, Canada
One Colomba Drive, Niagara Falls, New York 14305, U.S.A.

All rights reserved. No part of this book may be reproduced or transmitted in any form or by any means, electronic or mechanical, including photocopying and recording, or by any information storage or retrieval system, without permission in writing from the publisher.

Copyright © 1987 by Hayes Publishing Ltd.

ISBN 0-88625-171-0

Second Printing, 1992

CONTENTS

ANDREW CARNEGIE	4
BOB GELDOF	6
ALEXANDER GRAHAM BELL	9
MOTHER TERESA	12
CHARLES DARWIN	16
HENRY FORD	20
JOAN OF ARC	23
MAO TSE-TUNG	24
GOLDA MEIR	26
BOB HOPE	28
LUDWIG VAN BEETHOVEN	30
WALT DISNEY	34
JOE LOUIS	37
RICK HANSEN	39
ERNEST HEMINGWAY	42
WAYNE GRETZKY	46

ANDREW CARNEGIE

He was only fourteen years old at the time, but his small size and tow-headed shock of wavy, blonde hair made him look much younger. He climbed the long flight of wooden stairs two at a time, until he stood at the door of the great stone house. The boy reached up and seized the heavy knocker. He brought it down twice and waited. Moments later a servant appeared at the door.

"I'd like to borrow some books from Colonel Anderson, please," the boy asked with eager anticipation.

The servant led the boy inside. The house was richly decorated with famous paintings and expensive furniture. He paused before a large oak door.

"The librarian will be with you in a moment," said the servant.

The boy stared about the room. He had never seen so many books before in his life. He was in the home of Colonel James Anderson, a wealthy businessman who had built the first public library in Pittsburgh, Pennsylvania. The unsuspecting boy was in for a rude surprise."You cannot borrow any books here," the stern-faced librarian said, staring down at the boy from his rolltop desk. "You are not an apprentice."

An apprentice is a worker who is learning a trade such as carpentry or shoe making. Colonel Anderson insisted that only apprentices could use his library.

"But, sir," the young lad answered, "I'm a worker. I deliver telegraph messages in Pittsburgh."

The librarian snorted.

"You are not an apprentice," he said firmly. "Now get out."

Most boys would have hung their heads and walked away. But this was not an ordinary boy. This boy whom the librarian had turned away was destined to become one of the richest men in the world. He would become the biggest steel maker in the United States of America.

I'll write a letter to the editor of the newspaper, young Andrew Carnegie said to himself as he walked away from Colonel Anderson's home that day. And what a letter it was! The newspaper published it complete, and it caused quite a stir. Young Andrew complained of the stinginess of the rule allowing only apprentices to use the library. Within days he was invited to speak with the colonel himself. The old businessman liked this bold, young fellow. Here was a boy who could speak his mind! That very day the Anderson library of Pittsburgh, Pennsylvania, opened its doors to the general public. Andrew Carnegie had won another battle.

As a young immigrant boy from Dunfermline, Scotland, Andrew Carnegie had many battles to fight. His father was a poor man, earning a meager living as a cloth weaver. His mother helped by making shoes that she sold to a man who owned a shoe store. Andrew's family was so poor that he had to find a job when he was only thirteen years old. He would work all day long, delivering messages for the telegraph company in Pittsburgh and then come home at night and help his mother make shoes. He sat by her side threading needles and waxing the thread as she retold the stories and legends of his native Scotland. Andrew loved his mother very much. His one goal in life was to become a rich man so that he could make her life easier. In time he did both.

Andrew Carnegie owned many businesses in his lifetime. He introduced steel making to America at a time when few people believed in the future of steel. This was just after the American Civil War when people wanted to forget their troubles and rebuild the nation. Andrew Carnegie saw steel as the answer. He built bridges, railroads and factories out of steel. At first, people said it couldn't be done; cast iron was better, they said. Andrew knew otherwise. He never let other people discourage him. He set out to build the biggest steel company in the world near his new hometown of Pittsburgh, Pennsylvania. In no time at all the Carnegie mills were rolling out vast tonnages of steel every year and iron was used less and less. Iron cracked easily and was very heavy to lift. Steel was now king!

Andrew Carnegie never forgot the poverty of his youth. He wanted to return some of the blessings that America had given him. He gave over 60 million dollars for the construction of 2,800 public libraries all around the world. He knew the benefits of reading books. In addition, Andrew Carnegie financed numerous charitable organizations, including a five-million-dollar donation to the Hero Fund. This organization gave cash awards to people who had risked their lives during rescue attempts. The wealthy industrialist set up the Carnegie Institute in Washington with a 25 million-dollar grant. This agency works on scientific projects that help mankind. In 1905 he gave ten million dollars to set up the Carnegie Foundation for the Advancement of Teaching. Carnegie felt that teaching children was the most important job in the world. He wanted to help teachers do a good job and to provide pensions for them when they retired.

Andrew Carnegie died on August 11, 1919, at the age of 84. The former immigrant Scottish boy had given away over 340 million dollars to charitable causes. Though born into great poverty, this remarkable man set out to conquer the world. Armed with a firm belief in his ability to succeed, Andrew Carnegie became one of the wealthiest men of all time. In using his wealth to make life easier for other people, Andrew Carnegie showed the meaning of true greatness.

BOB GELDOF

The images on the TV screen were horrible - thousands of poor, starving Africans huddling outside the walls of a large building in Ethiopia, waiting for something to eat. Men, women and children, some so thin and weak from starvation they could barely stand, were anxiously waiting as the hot African sun beat down mercilessly, adding to their misery. A savage drought lasting for years had devastated Ethiopia, drying up the land and victimizing the people who lived on it. Scientists said it was one of the worst droughts they had ever seen. Some said it would last for years. The people were dying.

A man in England was watching television that day as the starving people of Africa waited for food. He couldn't believe what he was seeing. The pitiful conditions these poor people endured were worse than anything he could have imagined. Never had he seen such misery. He watched as a gate in the wall opened. Some people passed through and went inside the building. They were the lucky ones. They would each receive a small bowl of rice. Only 300 people went in that day. The gates shut on thousands more standing outside. The TV camera zeroed in on a thin little girl, no more than seven or eight years old, who had been shut out with the rest. Huge black flies buzzed about the little girl as she closed her eyes and leaned her head against the wall. After viewing this sorrowful scene, the man in England got up from his chair with tears in his eyes. He wiped the tears away with an angry swipe of his hand. Tears were not enough, he would later tell the world. Something had to be done. Bob Geldof would do something better.

Bob Geldof was born in the Dun Laoghaire neighborhood of Dublin, Ireland, in 1953. He was the youngest of three children. Bob's father was a textile merchant in the city. Bob's mother died when he was only six years old. Always a rebel, Bob nearly got expelled from school for promoting the writings of Chairman Mao. He left high school and worked as a bread deliveryman and a meat packer. It didn't seem as though Bob would ever make anything of his life. In 1975, Bob joined the Dublin-based rock band, The Boomtown Rats, as lead singer. The band enjoyed popular success, touring through England and Europe. They made several hit records that were heard on radio stations all around the world.

When Bob saw the starving little girl on television, he knew what he had to do. Together with a group of concerned British rock musicians, he co-wrote and produced the hit single *Do They Know It's Christmas*. This recording earned 11 million dollars in royalties. Bob saw to it that every cent went to African relief. He traveled to Ethiopia and talked to government officials. The money raised was used to buy food and farm equipment for the people. Wells were dug and water was found. It was a good start, but more was still needed.

Bob had another idea. He would put together two gigantic rock concerts -- one in England and the other in the United States -- and donate the proceeds to African relief. The concert was named *Live Aid*, and it would feature most of the top rock groups in the world. He rented the huge 72,000 seat Wembley Stadium outside London, England, and the J.F.K. Stadium in Philadelphia, Pennsylvania. Working day and night, Bob and his co-workers signed on rock stars like Stevie Wonder, Mick Jagger, Paul McCartney, Rod Stewart, Neil Young, U2, Dire Straits, Madonna and many other stars of the music world to play the concert. Each group would get twenty-two minutes to play four songs. The rock musicians agreed to donate every penny of the profit to African relief.

Live Aid opened on July 13, 1985. At Bob's invitation Prince Charles and Princess Diana attended the British concert. There was a live video hookup between the stadiums in England and America. Thousands of fans in both countries watched the huge screens as their favorite rock stars played, thousands of miles apart. Seven satellites beamed the concerts to over one hundred and sixty countries around the world. Millions of people, watching on television, were asked to phone in pledges of money to give to African relief. The lines were jammed with calls! So enthusiastic were the performers that one even played both concerts. After playing in England, Phil Collins flew to the United States on a Concorde and played there too!

Live Aid raised over one hundred million dollars which was placed in a special trust fund to provide relief for the drought victims in Africa. Geldof's idea had paid off. The sight of a suffering little girl in East Africa had given him a cause. Bob Geldof responded by organizing a stunning display of human brotherhood and generosity. Millions of people around the world were drawn closer together because of Bob Geldof's vision. Tears were not enough!

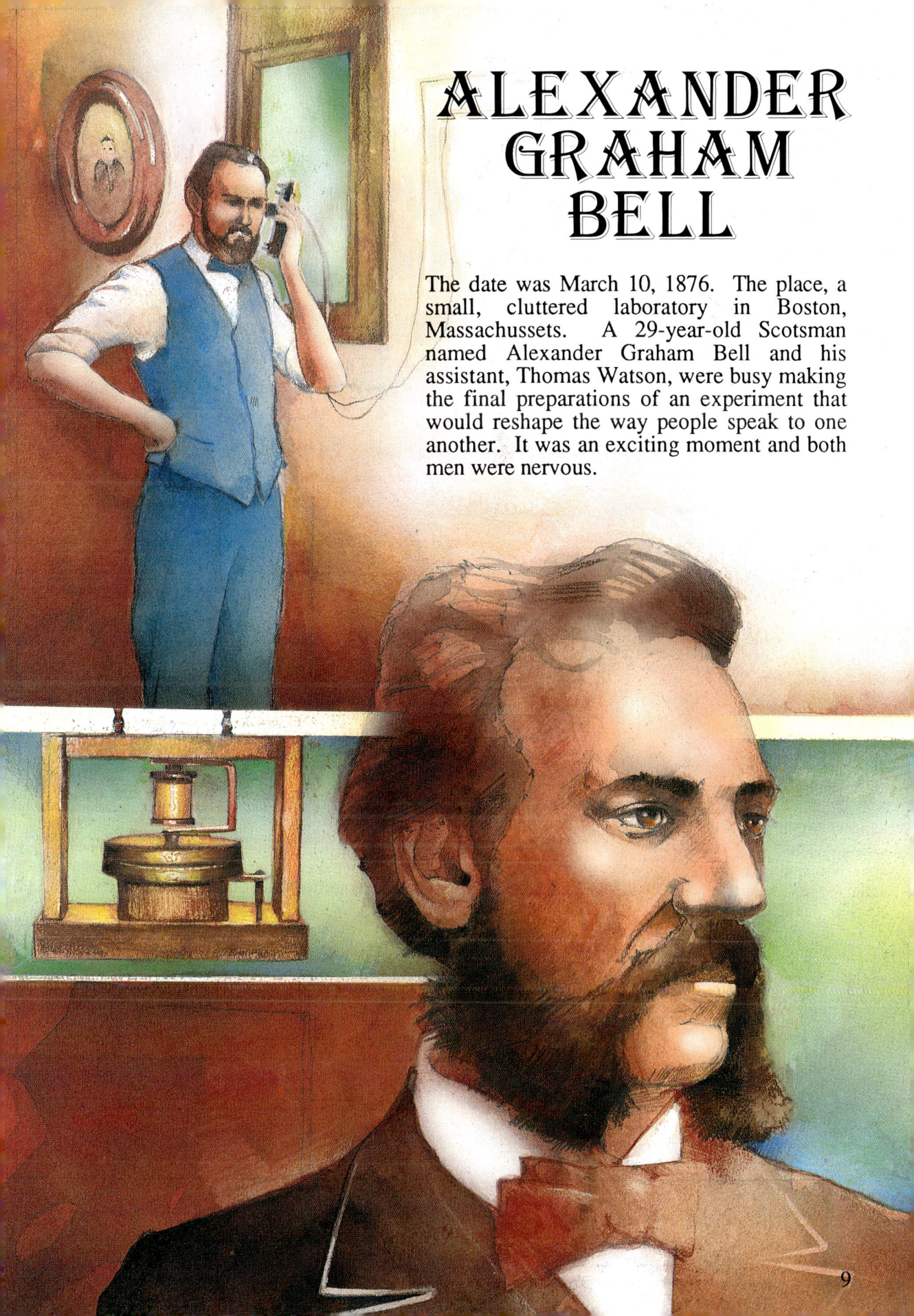

ALEXANDER GRAHAM BELL

The date was March 10, 1876. The place, a small, cluttered laboratory in Boston, Massachussets. A 29-year-old Scotsman named Alexander Graham Bell and his assistant, Thomas Watson, were busy making the final preparations of an experiment that would reshape the way people speak to one another. It was an exciting moment and both men were nervous.

Watson sat at a desk littered with batteries, wires and cables. Bell stood in another room off the laboratory, 60 feet away. Watson's receiver was attached to Bell's transmitter by a thin metal wire.

All was quiet inside the lab. Alexander began tinkering with the dials of his transmitter, when all of a sudden a beaker filled with acid fell off a shelf, spilling burning liquid all over his coat. The acid sizzled and sputtered, gouging great holes in the young man's clothing. Disregarding, for the moment, the experiment he was working on, Alex shrugged quickly out of his coat and called for help.

"Mr. Watson," he said, "come here. I want you."

Thomas Watson, sitting at his desk in a room 60 feet away, received the first telephone call of history!

It was an exciting moment -- the final triumph of years spent perfecting a method of sending the human voice along a thin, metal wire, and the young inventor hadn't even realized he had succeeded! Watson dashed into the room to find his friend shaking his head, upset about the spilled acid.

"Alex," Watson shouted excitedly, "I heard every word you said -- distinctly!"

Alexander Graham Bell didn't set out to invent the telephone. Born on March 3, 1847, in Edinburgh, Scotland, the future inventor was the son of Alexander and Eliza Grace Bell. Alexander's father was a famous teacher who had written a textbook on "visible speech" which was a code of symbols used to pronounce words in all languages. It involved the position of the tongue, lips and throat in producing certain sounds. Young Alex quickly learned to adapt visible speech to the needs of deaf people. He attended the University of Edinburgh where he studied to become a teacher. After graduation, Alex taught visible speech to deaf children in London, England.

Tragedy soon struck the Bell household. Edward, Alex's younger brother, had died several years earlier of tuberculosis. Now, in 1870, the eldest son, Melville, died of the same dreaded disease. Alexander's father knew what had to be done. The damp, cold climate of England was a threat to the health of his family. He immediately booked passage on a ship for the healthier climate of Canada, settling eventually in Brantford, Ontario.

Soon after their arrival in North America, Alexander's father received many requests to teach visible speech. He received a call from Miss Sarah Fuller, principal of a school for the deaf in Boston, Massachussets. The elder Bell had another engagement and could not go to Boston, so young Alex went in his place. He soon established himself at the Clarke School for the Deaf in Northampton, a small town outside Boston. Within a few weeks Alex had taught the children to use more than 350 syllables of English. This was truly amazing since the children had been struggling for years to learn these syllables.

In 1872, Alex opened a school for teachers of the deaf called the Vocal Physiology and Mechanics of Speech School in Boston. In 1873, Alex was invited to become a professor of voice at prestigious Boston University. At night, after teaching at the university all day, he would spend long hours in his basement laboratory trying to invent a machine that would telegraph human speech. He thought that his machine would help deaf children to hear and speak. Although he experienced great difficulty, and sometimes even failure, Bell knew that his machine could be built. He had strong faith that he could find the answer. At his home in Brantford, during summer holidays, young Alex would stretch out on the grass and dream of his "harmonic telegraph," as he called it. The clue that he was searching for was locked up inside the human ear.

After explaining his problem to a prominent American doctor, Bell received an interesting present -- a human ear! The doctor obtained the ear from a medical school and sent it to the young inventor. Alex slowly took the ear apart and studied it from the inside. He noticed that the thin membrane, called the eardrum, would tremble whenever he spoke. This trembling caused a series of small bones -- the anvil, hammer and stirrups - to move inside the ear. This movement was "decoded" by the brain into speech. The clue was discovered! In his laboratory, Bell constructed a thin, metallic plate, acting as an artificial eardrum, that was attached to a small strip of steel. He then ran an electric current through a wire that activated the steel and conducted sound waves to the plate. The telephone was invented!

For Alexander Graham Bell, the emergency telephone call of March 10, 1876, was the proof he needed to show the world that the human voice could be transmitted and received along a thin metal wire. Little did he know that his "harmonic telegraph" would one day be as common as the kitchen sink in most homes around the world. The invention of the telephone made Alexander Graham Bell a very rich man, but his first love was to the little deaf children who looked up to him as their teacher and friend.

Indeed, the life of this brilliant inventor shows us that love and concern for our fellow man are the very foundations of true genius.

Mother Teresa of Calcutta

On August 27, 1910, in the town of Skopje, Yugoslavia, a girl named Agnes Gonxha Bojaxhiu was born to an Albanian chemist and his wife. This little girl, who attended the government grammar school and grew up much like the other boys and girls of Yugoslavia, would have a meeting with destiny that would take place 36 years later in the large subcontinent of India. Her name, like everything else about her, would change. The little girl from Skopje, Yugoslavia, was destinated to become Mother Teresa of Calcutta.

Agnes Bojaxhiu joined the Roman Catholic convent of Our Lady of Loretto in Dublin, Ireland, on November 29, 1928. As a young girl, Agnes had read of the wonderful works of charity being performed in India by the sisters of the order. She arrived in India in 1928 and was sent to the wealthy city of Darjeeling. On January 6, 1929, the young novice, who took the religious name of Mary Teresa, arrived in the crowded city of Calcutta, home to lepers, beggars and the poorest of the poor as well as some of the wealthiest people in all of India. Sister Mary Teresa taught history and geography at St. Mary's High School from 1929 to 1948 and eventually became principal of the school.

One thing bothered the young nun. St. Mary's was an exclusive school, educating girls from only the very best Calcutta families. It took a great deal of money to attend St. Mary's. Just a few hundreds yards outside the neat, well-manicured lawns and gardens of the private school lived the poorest people of India, some so hungry and plagued with disease, they lay in the gutters of the street waiting to die. This contrast bothered Sister Mary Teresa as she went about her task of educating the privileged children of Calcutta.

On September 10, 1946, Sister Mary Teresa boarded a train for the city of Darjeeling where she attended her annual retreat. Again, the sights, sounds and smells of death and poverty surrounded her. Listening to the monotonous sound of the train wheels rolling over the steel rails, Sister Mary Teresa heard another voice, a voice she has since described as the "call of God" repeating to her over and over, "I must do something...I must do something...I must do something." That day marked Sister Mary Teresa's day of destiny. Determined to help India's poor, she returned to Calcutta and sought permission to leave her order. Permission was granted by Pope Pius XII, thus clearing the way for a new religious congregation - the Missionary Sisters of Charity. To the three vows of poverty, chastity and obedience, Sister Mary Teresa, now renamed Mother Teresa, added a fourth -- to serve the poorest of the poor of all creeds...to recognize God in the person of the poor, the unloved, the unwanted.

Mother Teresa began her work in earnest. With a handful of young, enthusiastic sisters, she started a small grammar school in the sprawling slum of Moti Jheel. Using only the hard-packed earth as a blackboard, Mother Teresa scratched out the daily lessons while her students -- children of the slum -- listened and learned. Her first task of the day was washing her pupils and attending to their medical needs. These children often came to Mother Teresa suffering from malnutrition. Many were infected with horrible diseases caused by polluted water and undercooked food. Also, the slum of Moti Jheel was crawling with huge rats that attacked the people as they slept. These bites usually caused terrible infections and often death.

In 1952, as Mother Teresa was walking through the narrow streets and alleyways of Calcutta searching for people in need of help, she found an old lady lying in the gutter outside a large hospital. The old lady was dying and was covered with hundreds of stinging black ants. Mother Teresa bent down and lifted the poor woman out of the gutter. She carried her into the hospital where she demanded a bed for the dying woman. The hospital staff refused to help. They said the old woman was too poor to pay for their services. Mother Teresa was furious. She refused to leave the hospital until the woman was given medical attention. The doctors finally permitted her to stay.

Mother Teresa never forgot the look of sorrow on the dying woman's face. It was a look of loneliness and despair. These people had nobody to care for them and nowhere to go. Mother Teresa asked the local government officials for a building where she could care for the dying poor of India. She was given an old building that once housed a Hindu temple. Mother Teresa renamed the building Nirmal Hriday, which means "Place of the Pure Heart." This was to be her home for the destitute and dying people of India. Many people were carried to Nirmal Hriday where they found a clean bed, good food and, most importantly, people who cared for their needs.

These poor people were able to die in peace, knowing that, at last, someone in this world had loved them.

In India, leprosy is a major problem. Over three million Indians have this dreaded disease, where huge sores cover the body and become so severe the person soon dies. Mother Teresa was determined to do something about this. She set about to build Shantinagar -- City of Peace -- a permanent refuge for lepers. At Shantinagar, a person with leprosy can live and receive medical aid. It has been estimated that Mother Teresa and her sisters have treated well over one and a half million lepers in India. Most people are afraid to come near a person with leprosy, but Mother Teresa knows this is wrong. Her motto for Shantinagar is simple - touch a leper, touch him with love.

Mother Teresa's work continues today in India and all around the world. The co-workers of Mother Teresa are an international organization of men and women serving the poor of this world. They belong to all faiths and to all walks of life. The people of India today are grateful to this tiny nun who one day heard the inspirational call to do something for her fellowman, and willingly answered the call.

CHARLES DARWIN

It was a warm summer day, unusually warm and muggy for England, and the young college student was tired. He had tramped many miles through the woods surrounding his beloved Cambridge University in search of rare beetles. He came to the bank of a small river stream and sat down. He felt so tired and worn out. Collecting insects was a tough job. He dangled his bare feet in the cool running stream and looked around. These woods were enormous. They must hold the rare beetles that he was searching for. He knew he had to keep looking in order to find them. He couldn't afford to waste time sitting by a stream. So the young man got up, stretched, put on his shoes and set off again.

It wasn't long before he found what he was looking for -- an old decayed tree trunk, half fallen over, covered with long strands of damp, green moss. The young college student pushed his way through the thick underbrush and stood by the tree. He seized a chunk of loose bark and ripped it away. Two huge black beetles clung to the sides of the trunk. The young man quickly grabbed both beetles, one in each hand, and examined them. They were perfect! Just the specimens he was looking for. He was about to turn and start back for school when something caught his eye. A large pair of thick, black antennae poked out through the torn bark. Another beetle! He stood there, watching the huge insect squirm itself out. It was a completely different kind of beetle than the two he held in his hand, with strange red markings on its back. He had to have it! But what could he do? Both hands were clasped tightly around the other two beetles, and he couldn't put them down for fear of losing them. He had to act quickly. The new, rare beetle was pushing itself back inside the bark. It was now or never! Without another thought the young man quickly popped one of the beetles into his mouth and grabbed the new beetle off the tree. He was so excited by his good luck that he didn't notice the strange sensation in his mouth. It wasn't until several seconds later that he felt it. The beetle in his mouth had ejected a burning, acid fluid. The young man gagged, spitting out the insect and the horrible burning liquid. In his excitement, he dropped the other two beetles and watched as they scurried quickly through the grass. It was another setback for the young college student, Charles Darwin.

Darwin was born in the town of Shrewsbury, England, on February 12, 1809. His father, a medical doctor, always encouraged young Charles to do his best. It was a great disappointment for his father that Charles did poorly at school. The subjects taught at that time included Greek, Latin and philosophy. Charles disliked these subjects. His real love was science. As a boy, young Charles spent many hours out in the woods or roaming the shore by the sea, collecting insects, spiders, shells and flowers. He would take his specimens home and mount them on wooden shelves. He loved to study the differences in all the things he found.

In time, Charles went to Cambridge University to study religion. While at Cambridge, he carried on with his scientific research, much to the displeasure of his father. Everyone at Cambridge knew that Charles was a good scientist. It was no wonder then that in 1831, at the age of 22, Charles decided to leave school and applied as a member of a ship's crew on a voyage that would take him around the world. The ship was HMS *Beagle*, commanded by a young navy officer, Captain Robert FitzRoy. Charles was officially commissioned as Ship's Naturalist. His job was to collect specimens of plants, animals and rocks from all around the world. The *Beagle* left Plymouth Harbor, England, on December 27, 1831, and sailed around the world. It didn't return to England until five years later, docking at Falmouth on October 2, 1836. In all that time Charles collected specimens and made notes.

One of the most interesting places that Darwin and the crew of the *Beagle* visited was the Cape Verde Islands off the coast of Africa in the Atlantic Ocean. Darwin noticed that thousands of cuttlefish were left stranded on the wet mud of the beach at low tide. The amazing thing about these fish was that, left out of water, they didn't die. Sailors eagerly left the *Beagle* in life boats and rowed to shore in anticipation of an easy harvest. As they bent over to scoop up the stranded fish, they got a hard squirt of water right in the face. Darwin was amazed. Here was a species of fish that had not only learned how to survive on dry land, but had also developed an effective method of self-defense against predators that might do them harm on the beach. This learned behavior enabled the cuttlefish to survive in its environment.

Another interesting stopover was the Galapagos Islands in the Pacific Ocean, off the coast of Ecuador. These islands were formed over 80 million years ago by a huge volcano that erupted out of the ocean floor. Black lava rock covers the desolate, windswept islands. One of the most unusual life forms on the Galapagos Islands is the three-foot-long iguana lizards. These lizards look like tiny dinosaurs. In fact, scientists trace their origin back to prehistoric times. Darwin was surprised, when he cut open the stomach of an iguana he had caught, to find chewed-up seaweed that was not found along the shoreline. Where had the iguana found this strange seaweed? Darwin soon got his answer. He watched in amazement as the lizards leaped off their black lava rocks into the sea and disappeared beneath the waves. In no time at all they reappeared, trailing long strands of seaweed in their mouths. The iguana had somehow overcome their fear of the sea and had learned how to swim and dive underwater to find food. Again, Darwin made notes and collected specimens.

He brought his collection home to England and began work on his great new book *The Origin of the Species*. He was greatly impressed with the variety of life forms in different parts of the world. Especially impressive was the way living creatures adapted to their environments. (To adapt means to make changes to new situations.) Charles noted that many of his rock samples contained fossils. A fossil is an ancient plant or bone that becomes embedded and preserved in rock millions of years old. These fossils were all different from one another. Each one represented an adaptation to a particular environment that changed over millions of years. As the environment changed, the living creatures changed. But what happened to those creatures that would not adapt to their changing environment? Darwin concluded that death wiped them all out. He called this process "natural selection." Nature selects only those life forms that can withstand changes and survive. Other people called this "survival of the fittest."

Charles Darwin challenged many beliefs and attitudes about life with his startling new book. He was critized by people who said that he was rejecting God and the Biblical view of life. But the great scientist denied that. He was a man who simply questioned fixed beliefs about how life on earth began and then set out, through his discoveries on the *Beagle*, to find answers. Today, most people believe in the Theory of Evolution, as Darwin's ideas are now called. Despite setbacks and constant criticism, this great scientist pushed ahead, opening up new frontiers of thought and knowledge that have come to be accepted all around the world.

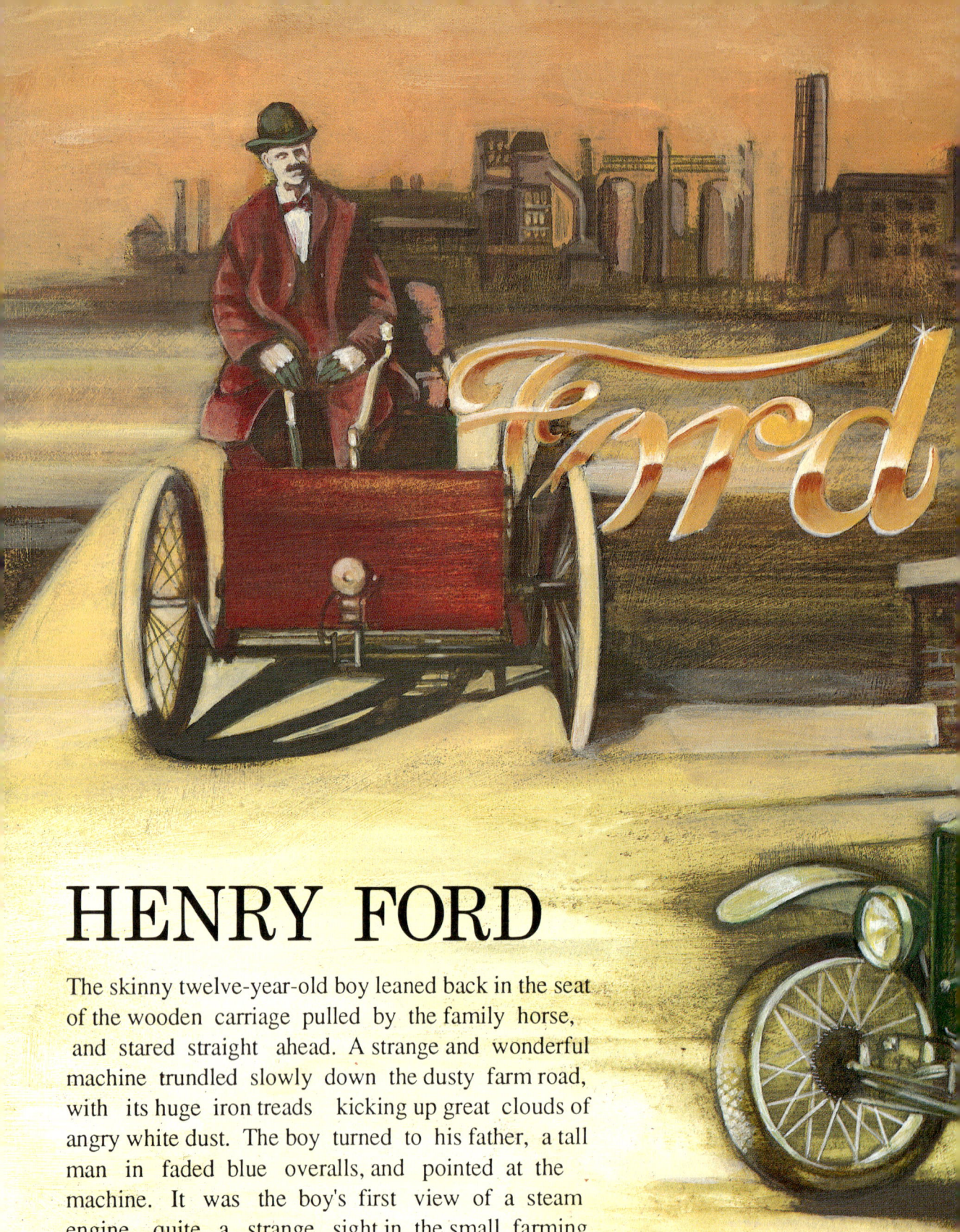

HENRY FORD

The skinny twelve-year-old boy leaned back in the seat of the wooden carriage pulled by the family horse, and stared straight ahead. A strange and wonderful machine trundled slowly down the dusty farm road, with its huge iron treads kicking up great clouds of angry white dust. The boy turned to his father, a tall man in faded blue overalls, and pointed at the machine. It was the boy's first view of a steam engine, quite a strange sight in the small farming village of Dearborn, Michigan, in the year 1875. The boy was amazed!

The man stopped the carriage and let his son out for a closer look. The boy ran, barefoot, through the soft, powdery dust and stood beside the machine. It was huge! The wheels, taller than the boy, were made of heavy cast iron. Clouds of hot white steam erupted from the valves at the top of the boiler. He heard the sound of boiling water growling inside the machine; the heat coming off the heavy steel plates almost knocked him over. It was all so wonderful. Yet, even as he stood fascinated by all the dials and valves, the boy knew something was wrong. The machine was used to help with farm work, but it just seemed too big to do an efficient job. It was also very expensive. Even though he was only twelve years old, young Henry Ford knew that he could build a better engine.

Although he was born in the country, Henry Ford had no intention of being a farmer. He was very handy at fixing things, and often spent long hours tinkering with machines. He even started a little business, repairing watches and clocks for the neighboring farmers. With the money earned, young Henry bought parts for the new engine he was developing. It would run on gasoline and would be much smaller and cheaper than the steam engine. It was called the internal combustion engine, and it would change the way people traveled.

In time, Henry Ford moved to the nearby city of Detroit. His dream was to create a gasoline engine that could propel a carriage along a road without the benefit of a horse. People thought that Henry Ford was crazy and that his "horseless carriage" idea was just a dream. Ford didn't care what people thought; he knew it could be done. He had learned, as a boy on the farm, that anything was possible if you only believed in yourself and worked hard.

In no time at all, Henry Ford developed his "horseless carriage." He took a standard horse-and-buggy carriage and made a few changes. Underneath the seat he placed his new gasoline engine. Imagine the look of surprise when Ford drove his strange machine through the streets of Detroit for the first time! People were astonished; the amazing contraption actually worked!

Henry Ford refined his idea of a horseless carriage and eventually went into production of the model T Ford and went on to build the world's largest automotive factory at Highland Park, Michigan. He employed thousands of men to put his cars together along an assembly line. Each man had one job to do. For example, one man put the doors on a car, while another man worked on the engine. The assembly line churned out thousands of "horseless carriages" every year. In fact, Henry Ford's huge automobile plant could produce one car every minute of every day of the year. This was called mass production. Ford decided, early in his career, that it would be better to mass produce thousands of average-priced cars rather than custom-build a few very expensive cars. This was a wise decision. People all over the country could afford to pay for Henry Ford's mass-produced cars. They were very inexpensive, yet well-built.

Henry Ford became one of the richest men in the world. It was a long, hard road from the simple country farm in Dearborn, Michigan, to the huge automobile factory in Highland Park. Yet, like so many other marvellous people, Ford started out with a dream. To make his dream come true, he had to believe in himself. Henry Ford always believed that he could make an inexpensive, efficient gasoline engine that most people could afford. Even when others doubted him and thought he was wasting his time, Ford believed in his dream. When a person believes in himself, great things are possible!

Joan of Arc

She was a mere girl of thirteen when the voices began to speak to her. She seemed to be in a trance, a pleasant smile lighting up her plain, young face. The girl told people that the voices commanded her to go to the dauphin and help save France from the English. The daupin was the son of the king of France. France and England were at war with each other. The young girl said the voices told her to lead the French soldiers to victory. People just smiled and shook their heads. How could young Joan of Arc ever lead an army to war?

Joan was born near the village of Domremy, France, in 1411. She often prayed to her favorite saints, Saint Catherine, Saint Michael and Saint Margaret. She was very kind to animals, and rabbits, birds and deer would come up to Joan and eat out of her hand.

When she was eighteen, Joan left her father's house and went to see the daupin. Joan told the daupin to have hope; she would lead the French soldiers to victory.

Wearing shining white armor and riding a black horse, Joan led an army of French soldiers against the English at the city of Orleans. A long, fierce battle took place, and the English army was driven out of Orleans.

People started to say that Joan had used witchcraft against the English at Orleans. They couldn't understand how such a young girl could be so successful in war. Now they were calling her a witch. The English persuaded the French people to arrest Joan and put her on trial. The court condemned Joan to die. She was tied to a pole that was piled up, on the ground, with wood. The wood was lit and Joan was burned to death. She had fought to save France from the English soldiers, but now she had died at the hands of the people she had saved!

In 1920, Joan of Arc was made a saint of the Roman Catholic Church.

It was called The Long March. One hundred thousand soldiers and 6,000 miles of rugged land. The orders were simple -- start walking.

The year was 1934. China was gripped by a massive civil war. The Kuomintang Party, led by General Chiang Kai-Shek, wanted to establish a new national government for China. General Chiang was opposed by a man who had once taught grade school in his native province of Hunan in Central China. His name was Mao Tse-tung.

Mao was 41 years old and the leader of the Chinese Communist Party when the Long March began. General Chiang's forces had encircled Mao's troops near their base in Kiangsi Province. Under the cover of night, Mao's soldiers broke out. They left Kiangsi and marched away from the Kuomintang troops. Constant fighting took place and thousands of men died.

The worst part of the Long March was the trek through the Grasslands. This was a horrible swampy region of China, stretching from the frightening Great Snow Mountain. Hailstones pounded Mao and his men as they left the heights and descended to the swamp. The worst, however, was yet to come. The Grasslands were more water than land. Dark, muddy streams flowed inches beneath the long, reedy grass. Swarms of mosquitoes attacked the men. Huge, black leeches crawled onto their legs and sucked their blood. To make matters worse, the water was poisonous, causing ugly sores on their bodies. Ropes were tied from man to man to keep everyone together in the thick white fog hanging inches above the grass. Sometimes, a man would step into a section of quicksand and disappear into the earth, pulling all of his friends in with him. Mao's army managed to break loose from the nightmare swamp and pushed on toward their destination of Shensi where they arrived exactly twelve months after leaving Kiangsi Province. Mao became a legend to the Chinese people, strengthening his position, especially with the peasant farmers living in the country. These people, who had helped Mao during the Long March, now listened to him as he told them about communism.

Mao's father was a wealthy farmer who treated people worse than animals. He would whip a man if he disobeyed his orders. Mao could have stayed on the family farm and become a rich man, but he had other plans. He wanted to help people in some way. Mao decided to become a school teacher.

Communism teaches that wealth is bad for a person. Mao believed this. He felt that people must give up their private property and share their wealth.

After World War II, the Kuomintang forces were defeated by Mao's Red Army. In 1949, Mao became the first Chairman of the People's Republic of China. He was now known as Chairman Mao.

Many people disagree with communism. They protest the lack of freedom in countries like China and Russia. People in these countries are forbidden to own private property or to acquire wealth. Nevertheless, Mao Tse-tung was a great leader. This remarkable man took control of a huge country, the second largest in the world, with a population approaching one billion people, and welded it into a powerful nation. He turned his back on riches and an easy life to do something useful for China. The battles with the Kuomintang and the struggle during the Long March had toughened his spirit. Chairman Mao deserves the title Father of Modern Day China.

25

golda meir

How many people would leave the comfort of a safe, warm home secure in the knowledge that they could walk their city streets, even at night, without fear of attack or arrest? Or who would give up a way of life that guaranteed material happiness and comforts as well as a good-paying job? Not many. And when you then ask who would give up all of this to travel thousands of miles across the ocean to another land that was hardly more than a swamp surrounded by a vast desert, with fierce enemies on every side, you might not even get an answer. Yet one person did all of this. The day was May 23, 1921, in New York City. A slender 23-year-old school teacher boarded the SS *Pocahontas* and turned to wave a final goodbye to the United States of America. Golda Meir was bound for Palestine.

Golda Meir was born Golda Mabovitch in Kiev, Russia, on May 3, 1898, the daughter of a Jewish carpenter. In Russia, little Golda had seen much hatred and violence. Jews were beaten up and sometimes killed because they had a different religion and language than the other people. A drunken man once came up to little Golda and her seven-year-old playmate, grabbed their hair and knocked their heads together. As the little girls fell to the ground, the man laughed and said that the Jews would get more of that if they stayed in Russia. Angry mobs rampaged through Jewish neighborhoods, smashing doors and windows and setting buildings on fire. This was called a pogrom. Golda's parents decided to move to America where they could raise their children in peace.

The Mabovitch family eventually settled in Milwaukee, Wisconsin, where Golda earned good grades at school. She decided to become a teacher. She also became a Zionist. A Zionist was a person who wanted to see Palestine returned as a national homeland for the Jews. The Zionists argued that Jews had lived for centuries in Palestine. In the year 70 A.D., a Roman army had driven all the Jews out of Palestine and dispersed them throughout Europe and Asia. Now, the Jews wanted to go back home.

Golda made a tough decision. She would leave America and go to Palestine. There she would help to rebuild the Jewish national homeland.

It was hard work for the young school teacher and her husband, Morris. Roads had to be built, swamps drained and trees planted. The desert lay all around them. Also, the Arabs who lived in the countries surrounding Palestine did not like to see the Jews returning to their old homeland. They fought many battles against the Jews. But the young people, like Golda, fought back and refused to leave.

On May 14, 1948, Golda took part in the signing of the Proclamation of Independence that established the Jewish nation of Israel. The dream had come true! After more than 2,000 years of wandering around the world, the Jews had finally come home! But many trials lay ahead. The Arab nations were more determined than ever to destroy the Jews. More fighting took place, with great loss of life.

Two great conflicts with her Arab neighbors loomed ominously in the future -- the Six Day War in 1967 and the Yom Kippur War in 1973. In both cases, Israel was fighting for her very life. The Arab nations such as Egypt, Syria and Jordan, were determined to wipe the State of Israel off the face of the map. These nations opposed the formation of the Jewish state in the Middle East. In both wars, however, Israel emerged victorious, thanks in part to the determined leadership of Golda Meir.

Golda served as Israel's Minister of Labor from 1949 to 1956 and as Minister of Foreign Affairs from 1956 to 1966. In 1969 she became Prime Minister of Israel until her retirement in 1974.

The Israeli people loved Golda. As one of the first Jewish pioneers in Palestine, she had labored hard to build the homeland they had dreamed about. Giving up a good home and prosperous lifestyle in America to come to the wilderness of Palestine in 1921 was a tough decision to make. For Golda Meir, though, the decision was really quite simple. The Jewish people needed her help. She never let them down.

Bob Hope

Life is tough for a boy at the best of times, but his first name made it seem even tougher. Leslie. The kids at school laughed whenever they heard his name.

The little boy with the English accent fought back with his fists. It wasn't his fault that his parents had given him a girl's name. He would show the bullies in his class. He wouldn't let them push him around.

In time, the little boy named Leslie became a good boxer. Fighting under the name Packie East, he turned semi-pro at the age of eighteen. He thought that boxing would be his key to success, but he was wrong. Young Leslie Hope felt the call of something even stronger -- show business!

Bob Hope was born Leslie Townes Hope on May 29, 1903, in the quiet English village of Eltham. His family moved to America in 1908, settling in Cleveland, Ohio, where Bob's father, William, worked as a stonemason. Hard times, however, soon fell upon the Hope household. William turned to drinking when his business failed. Bob's mother, Avis, encouraged her boys to do their best. She told them that America was the land of opportunity for those who work hard.

Leslie, who changed his name to Bob, went on to become a dancer and comedian in vaudeville. Vaudeville was an early form of theater in which the actors and actresses would dance, tell jokes and sing songs before live audiences. Bob traveled across the United States with many vaudeville companies. From vaudeville, Bob signed up with the great theaters of Broadway in New York City. He was only 24 years old. He appeared in many productions featuring the top stars of the nineteen twenties and thirties, rubbing shoulders with Eddie Cantor, Jimmy Durante and Fred Astaire. In 1930, Bob moved west, attracted by the movie industry in Hollywood, California. He has acted in 73 films including *Bachelor in Paradise, Call me Bwana, The Lemon Drop Kid* and *Paris Holiday*. Perhaps the most successful Hope movies were the famous *Road* films with Bob's good friends, Bing Crosby and Dorothy Lamour. The first *Road* film was *The Road to Singapore* which premiered in April, 1940. In time, seven *Road* films were made. These films were set in exotic foreign countries with Bob and Bing trying to win the hand of the beautiful Lamour while keeping one step ahead of a crowd of nasty villains. Audiences loved the *Road* films. They were just the thing to lift the spirits of America as World War II loomed ahead.

During the war, Bob Hope became a symbol of America to the U.S. soldiers stationed overseas. On Christmas Day, 1942, Bob assembled a staff of show business people to fly to U.S. bases and entertain the troops. Bob took his Christmas Show to the soldiers in the Korean and Vietnam wars as well. He never stopped caring for the men who fought so hard so that other men could be free. Bob put his own life on the line many times during these shows. He visited the sick and wounded in the mobile hospitals and gave comfort to the dying. He would often jot down the telephone numbers of wounded G.I.s and call their parents when he returned to the States. It was all part of Bob's message of love and concern that filled so much of his life.

Today, Bob Hope is a living legend, included among the greats of Hollywood. His optimistic sense of humor has gotten America through some pretty tough scrapes. People have learned to forget their troubles for a while and laugh at Bob's famous one-liners. His movies have lightened the hearts of many made heavy with fear and sorrow.

LUDWIG VAN BEETHOVEN

In the summer of 1802, in the beautiful hardwood forest surrounding the village of Heiligenstadt, Austria, the greatest musician of Europe stood beside a large oak tree and gazed about. He was still a young man, barely 32 years old, yet already recognized as a musical genius. He had come to this tiny village to get away from all the noise and excitement of his home in Vienna. In that city, the young musician gave piano recitals before the kings and queens of Europe. He needed a rest from all of his efforts.

He had heard about the sulphur baths that abounded near Heiligenstadt. Sulphur baths were once thought to be helpful to people suffering from poor health. The young musician's health was not good. He hoped to find a cure in the warm mineral waters so that he could return to Vienna and continue with his musical career. He turned away from the tall oak tree and gazed down at a nearby meadow. A shepherd, playing a flute, stood in the field with his flock of sheep. The young musician immediately left the forest and approached the shepherd. He wanted to hear the music of the flute. He walked closer and closer, but still he heard nothing. The shepherd turned when he saw the young man approaching and stopped playing. The musician beckoned him to continue. The shepherd put the flute to his lips and played. Still the musician heard nothing. He was now standing beside the shepherd. Total silence! It was a crushing moment for the young musician, Ludwig van Beethoven. He now knew, for certain, that he was deaf.

Ludwig van Beethoven was born on December 16, 1770, in Bonn, Germany. His father, Johann, was a poor man who earned a meager living as a tenor singer at the court of the German Elector. The family lived in a poor section of Bonn. Ludwig was one of seven children, four of whom died at birth. Conditions in the Beethoven household were harsh. Johann turned to wine and beer to escape the poverty of his life. In an effort to make something of his family, Johann decided to teach young Ludwig to become a musician. He forced the boy, at the age of four, to practice the violin for several hours a day. Young Ludwig didn't like to play music. He often cried during these long, uninterrupted practices, but still he persisted. Ludwig performed his first public concert on March 26, 1778. He was only eight years old. In 1784, at the age of fourteen, Ludwig was hired as a deputy court organist in the orchestra of Maximilian Francis, son of Maria Theresa, the Empress Ruler of Austria. Life seemed better for the Beethoven family. Then tragedy struck. In 1787 Ludwig's mother died. This drove Ludwig's father to despair. Two years later, at the age of nineteen, Ludwig took responsibility for his two brothers, Karl, fifteen, and Johann, thirteen. In 1792, Ludwig's father died, leaving his three sons alone in the world.

Ludwig's musical abilities were noticed by many important people in Bonn. At their urging, he went to Vienna where he played the piano for Wolfgang Mozart, at that time the greatest musician in Europe. Mozart was very impressed with Beethoven. Here was a young man who would do great things in the world of music. In no time at all, the young musician from Bonn had a large following of people who paid great amounts of money to hear him play. Although short and stocky, with rough manners and a short temper, Beethoven made people love him whenever he sat before the piano and played. His bad temper often got him into trouble, though. Once, at a restaurant, a waiter brought the wrong food to Beethoven's table. The musician was furious. He yelled at the waiter and told him to take back the food. The waiter didn't like the way Beethoven spoke to him and yelled back at Beethoven. Without another word, the great musician stood up and dumped the plate of meat and gravy over the poor man's head.

Beethoven was a very proud man. He had to struggle through a childhood marked by poverty and an alcoholic father to learn all he could about music. It was not an easy life for a young boy, but Ludwig never gave up. He knew that one day he would be a great musician. He pushed himself as hard as he could to improve his playing ability. He once told a famous prince that a thousand princes would come and go after he was dead, but there would be only one Beethoven. People often misunderstood him when he talked like this. They thought he was being arrogant. Actually, Ludwig was reacting to the soft, privileged lifestyle of the very rich who never had to struggle to achieve success. He knew about poverty and hardship as a boy, but he never let this hold him down.

Perhaps the greatest tragedy in the life of this great musician was the loss of his hearing. This was a tragic loss, especially for a man who had dedicated his life to making beautiful sounds. It came on gradually, when he was in his early thirties. Eventually, Beethoven became completely deaf. He would never again hear the wonderful music that had made him famous. Most people would have despaired of ever again finding happiness. Not so of Ludwig van Beethoven. Instead, he turned his talents to composing music, spending the next 25 years creating magnificent symphonies and operas. Perhaps if he had never become deaf we would have never experienced his incredible works of art. Beethoven knew, after he became deaf, that he would never again play a musical instrument. This realization forced him to compose music, for his heart and soul were still on fire with the love of beautiful sounds.

When classifying music into time periods, it is customary to place Beethoven in the Classical period. This lasted from approximately 1750 to 1820 and is notable primarily for the large symphony orchestra that came into being at that time. Previously, music was written for the enjoyment of only a few people, usually the wealthy aristocrats. These people gathered in each other's homes to listen to small groups of musicians perform works that were intended for large public audiences. This was known as "chamber music." By the middle of the eighteenth century, however, the general public began to demand its share of the musical genius being reserved for the wealthy few. In time, larger groups of musicians performed in public halls before sold-out crowds of appreciative audiences. These public concerts demanded larger orchestras with greater ranges of power than ever before. New and better instruments were invented. A great musical genius had been set free. The great symphony orchestra came into being.

In response to this new spirit, Beethoven produced one of the greatest musical landmarks of all time - the *Eroica*. Eroica means "heroic," and it superbly reflects the theme of this great symphony. Beethoven wanted to create a musical testament to the new forces sweeping Europe. Human reason was considered the crowning achievement of mankind, the faculty shaping the will and destiny of the world. Equally important as human reason, however, was the faculty of creative emotion. Artists like Beethoven could lend creative force to human reason, charging a work of intellect with evermore powerful meanings.

The *Eroica* was performed for the first time on April 7, 1805, in the Theater-an-der-Wien in Germany. Beethoven, although deaf by this time, conducted the entire symphony himself. The reviews were not kind. Many people could not understand Beethoven's meaning in *Eroica*. They found the work harsh and clashing and even somewhat violent. It may be that Beethoven wanted his symphony to sound this way. The full title of *Eroica* -- "Heroic symphony to celebrate the memory of a great man" -- was dedicated to Napoleon Bonaparte, the Corsican general who later became Emperor of France.

Ludwig van Beethoven died on March 26, 1827. He was 57 years old. His symphonies, overtures, concertos and chamber music rank as among the very best music ever produced by man. Although born into crushing poverty and suffering the further hardship of the loss of his hearing, this remarkable man rose to the heights of musical fame. His legacy is found wherever beautiful music is heard.

WALT DISNEY

It was four-thirty in the morning, pitch black and freezing cold with a blizzard raging across the rugged Missouri farmlands. A lonely ten-year-old boy, dressed in a thin, patched overcoat with a woolen muffler wrapped tightly around his throat, leaned into the wind. The heavy bag of newspapers hanging at his side helped to anchor him against the storm. He was a delivery boy for the *Kansas City Star,* making his daily early-morning rounds. The streets were filling with snow as the blizzard roared through town. Kansas City would come to a standstill, but the *Kansas City Star* would still get out. The boy plodded along, despite the storm, getting the newspapers to every house on his route. The boy took pride in serving his customers. He knew that they depended on him. He wouldn't let them down. In later years, this same boy would remember those early mornings in Kansas City and the hardships he had to endure. Those early lessons would one day pay off for the man whose name became synonymous with quality entertainment -- Walt Disney.

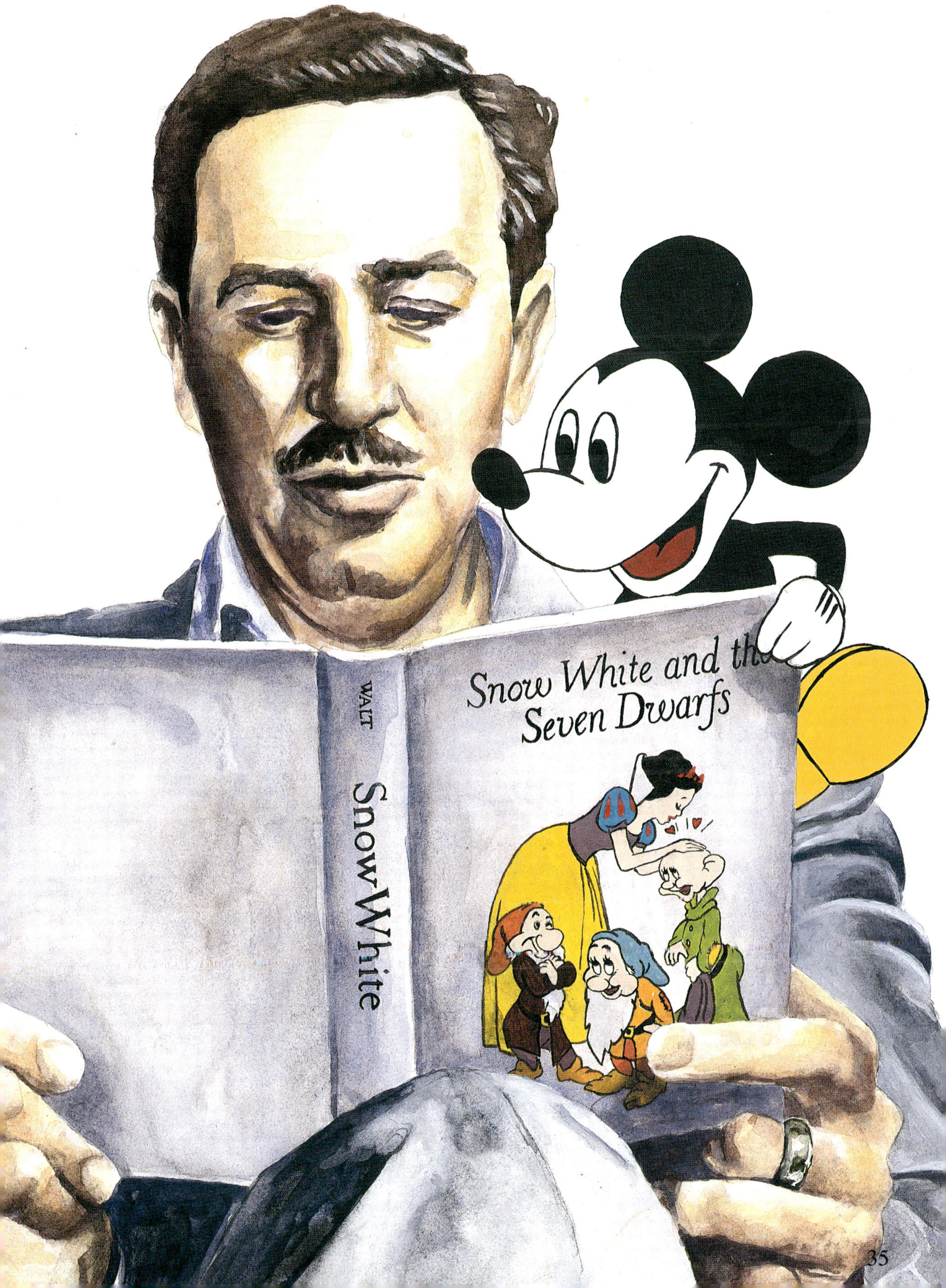
Snow White and th
Seven Dwarfs
WALT
Snow White

Walt Disney was born in 1901 on a farm in Marceline, Missouri. His father, Elias, was an apple farmer. Walt loved the farm, even though he had to work hard at his chores. Walt was a good artist even as a young boy. He always found time to sketch the animals, trees and orchards of his father's farm. But that all changed. The apple crop was no longer profitable. In 1910, Elias sold the farm and moved his family to Kansas City where young Walt got his first job delivering newspapers.

In 1920, at the age of nineteen, Walt started his own business. He had always been a good artist and liked to draw cartoons. He decided to make "animated" cartoons. To do this he filmed many drawings of the same character that were slightly moved to make it look as though the cartoon was animated or "alive." His first animated feature was called *Alice in Cartoonland.* Later, he produced *Oswald the Rabbit.* People liked these new cartoons. It looked like Walt was headed for success when disaster struck. The artists who had worked with Disney on these projects decided to leave Walt's company and start up on their own. They took the idea for Oswald with them. Walt couldn't do a thing about it. He returned to his new home in California, determined to start all over again.

In his office, he toyed with a new cartoon character. Oswald was gone, but maybe the public would like a cartoon about a mouse. Walt remembered his early days in Kansas City as a young artist. A tiny mouse that he had nicknamed Mortimer allowed Walt to feed him crumbs from his lunch. In time, Mortimer became quite tame and performed tricks for his master. Walt now remembered Mortimer. He renamed his new cartoon character *Mickey Mouse.* This tiny character propelled Walt Disney back on the road to success.

In 1935, Walt made the first full-length cartoon movie. It was called *Snow White and The Seven Dwarfs* and was a huge success. Some people told Walt that *Snow White* would fail. They didn't think that children would sit through a full-length cartoon movie. Walt proved them wrong. *Snow White* became the most popular cartoon movie ever made. After World War II, Walt produced three more cartoon movies - *Cinderella, Alice in Wonderland* and *Peter Pan.* In 1949, Walt made his first movie, *Treasure Island,* which thrilled audiences everywhere. Since then the Disney studios have made several full-length movies, famous for their clean-cut sense of fun and adventure.

Perhaps Walt's biggest gamble was his huge theme amusement park, Disneyland. As the father of two small girls, Walt was disappointed by the dirtiness of the amusement parks they visited. He wanted to build the world's biggest, cleanest park with rides and attractions that could be both fun and educational. He invested millions of dollars in a 160-acre parcel of land near Anaheim, California, and opened his "Magic Kingdom" to the world in 1955. It was a huge success. So many people visited the California Disneyland that Walt built another on the other side of the country near Orlando, Florida.

Today, millions of people pass through the gates of both Disneylands. There, they find monuments to the genius of a man who knew great adversity in his life but who never gave up. From a poor ten-year-old paper boy, trudging through the snow-choked streets of Kansas City, to the multi-millionaire moviemaker, Walt Disney always believed in himself. He knew that people depended on him to do a good job. He never let them down.

JOE LOUIS

The crowd at Yankee Stadium was tense with excitement. More than 70,000 people crammed the "house that Babe built" to see the fight. It was more than just a boxing match, though. The men in brown shirts surrounding the ring, wearing the black and white Nazi swastika on their left armbands, would see to that. They were Adolf Hitler's propaganda crew, anxiously awaiting the expected outcome of this fight between German Max Schmeling and the "Brown Bomber," American Joe Louis.

It was a warm New York night on June 22, 1938, as millions of people around the world leaned closer to their radios to listen to the greatest fight of the decade. It was seen as a battle between the American democratic way of life and the ugly brutality of German Nazism.

The Nazis were a small group of people who believed that Germans were superior people. Not everyone in Germany believed this. Unfortunately, the Nazis seized power in Germany and their leader, Adolf Hitler, forced the people to accept this belief. In time, Hitler led the German people to war with the rest of the world. In 1938, however, Adolf Hitler only wanted one thing. He wanted Max Schmeling to beat Joe Louis and prove to the world that the German people were superior.

37

Louis and Schmeling had trained hard. They were very close in weight -- 198 pounds for Louis and 193 for Schmeling. They had run many miles and sparred against many opponents to get in shape for this fight. It was now or never. Louis, led by a platoon of New York City policemen, crossed the field of Yankee Stadium under the glare of the lights. He was wearing a red and blue robe that looked, to many people, like the American flag. Seventy thousand fight fans jumped from their seats and let out a mighty roar. Next came Schmeling, wearing a light gray robe. The crowd grew tense. Both men entered the ring and skipped around, throwing light jabs at the air. The referee called the fighters to center ring. He gave his instructions, cautioning against low blows. The Nazi broadcaster, Arno Helmers, hunched over his radio microphone and beamed the news back to Germany. Helmers wanted Schmeling to win. He believed it would happen.

The bell sounded and both fighters left their corners. Louis stared at his opponent. He didn't care that Schmeling was a Nazi. He was just another boxer. The Brown Bomber jabbed twice at the German's face, backing Schmeling against the ropes. A Louis left hook, followed by a thundering right cross to the jaw staggered his opponent. Schmeling looked dazed. Arno Helmers stopped his broadcast in mid-sentence. Now Schmeling came at Louis, but his guard was down. Louis hit him with a left, then a right to the jaw again. Schmeling dropped to his knees. The referee began the count. One, two, three. But the German, dazed and slightly bleeding, got back up from the canvas. Louis moved in for the kill. He hit Schmeling once more. This time the German stayed down. The referee counted to five before stopping the fight. It was all over! After only two minutes into the first round, the great Nazi fighter was out cold!
The referee raised Joe Louis' arm in victory. The crowd went wild.

Life wasn't always a victory for Joe Louis. Born Joe Louis Barrow in a small log cabin near Lafayette, Alabama, on May 13, 1914, his parents were poor sharecropper farmers. In the southern United States many people who were too poor to own their own farms had to rent land from someone else. In return for the use of the land, the sharecropper gave up a part of his crop to the landowner. Life was hard for Joe Louis and his family. His father and mother were children of former black slaves. Many white people at that time hated black people. This is called racial prejudice. Joe Louis didn't care. He worked hard in the field, planting and picking cotton and chopping wood. When he was a young boy, Joe's father got sick and went into a hospital. Joe never saw his father again. He had to work twice as hard as before, helping his mother with chores around the house. His mother depended on Joe and he never let her down. She told him that a good name is better than riches and always urged her son to do the right thing. Joe loved and respected her because of her optimistic outlook on life. Later, when the family moved to Detroit, Joe found work in the automobile factories. It was in Detroit that Joe Louis learned to box. He would work all day long at the Ford factory and then box at night at the Brewster Center, a local athletic club. His mother told Joe to do his best at boxing if that was what he really wanted to do. Again, Joe followed her advice. From 1935 to 1949, Joe Louis won 37 of 38 fights. He won the heavyweight championship in 1937 and defended his title 25 times during the next twelve years.

Joe Louis was a great American athlete. Although born into great poverty and hardship, he worked at the sport he loved and became the greatest boxer in the world. Joe's mother was a big influence on his life. She always reminded Joe that he was just as good as anyone else and that he should be the best he could be. Joe Louis proved to the world that the championship spirit exists in people who truly believe in themselves.

RICK HANSEN

Up and down, up and down, 75 strokes a minute, 4,500 strokes an hour, 36,000 strokes a day, Rick Hansen, the wheelchair athlete, is pushing himself around the world. His days begin with the quiet of the dawn as he fulfills this dream. Rick's journey to help victims of spinal cord injuries is often a very difficult one. However, it's been no more difficult than having undergone his own journey back to health and strength. Rick's personal commitment and desire keep him rolling with enthusiasm and fire into a new dawn.

Rick Hansen, 28, was a star athlete at high school before tragedy struck in June, 1973. Rick was fifteen years old when he and a buddy, Don Adler, were hitching a ride home from a fishing trip in the back of a pickup truck. The truck rolled on a corner, and a large steel box slammed into Rick's lower back. He suffered a spinal cord injury and was paralyzed from the waist down.

Initially, Rick was very depressed. His life, as he had known it, was over, and this was very hard for him to accept. However, thanks to the help of an older paraplegic who introduced Rick to wheelchair sports, he found a new direction.

Rick met other wheelchair athletes and began to push himself harder and harder to achieve top physical condition. Since then, Rick has won many awards for his great strength and skill. He was named Canada's Disabled Athlete of the Year in 1979, 1980 and 1982; was co-winner, with Wayne Gretzky, of the Lou Marsh Trophy for Canada's outstanding athlete in 1983; he has been a three-time winner of the world wheelchair marathon title, and has won fifteen other individual marathons. In 1982, Canada could not have been prouder of Rick. He took home a record nine gold medals in Halifax at the Pan American Games for the Disabled.

While working on a physical education degree at the University of British Columbia in Vancouver, Rick played basketball and volleyball on a team with Terry Fox. A close relationship developed between the young men.

It was then that Rick started feeling he could do more for the disabled, especially victims of spinal cord injuries as this is an area where great potential exists to find methods that will help people walk again.

In pursuit of this, Rick rolled out of Vancouver, British Columbia, with a great dream to become the first man to wheel around the world. This was Rick's way of calling the world's attention to the plight of so many disabled who are in wheelchairs due to spinal cord injuries. Rick knows there is great potential to find a way to get these disabled out of their wheelchairs and walking again. What is needed is the financial support that governments and research programs could give the spinal cord injury cause. With this support a cure is that much closer. Rick's precious personal goal is his burning desire to demonstrate to other handicapped people, government aid and research agencies that the capabilities of the wheelchair-bound are limitless.

Rick's quest is known as *The Man in Motion World Tour*. At its completion, he will have traveled 40,073 km -- the distance around the world at the equator. He has traveled from Vancouver, Canada, down the west coast of the United States to California, across the American deserts to the Atlantic east coast and overseas to Britain. He and his six-man team then moved on through Europe and down to Australia and New Zealand. He then went on to cover Japan, China and Korea. Next, Rick flew back to the east coast of the United States to Florida where he wheeled his way up through the eastern seaboard to Nova Scotia and started the last leg of his journey through Canada, which in itself is over 11,000 km.

Altogether, Rick has traveled through 34 countries around the world, and everywhere he's traveled his *Man in Motion World Tour* has struck a note of goodwill and unity. Wherever Rick and his crew went they needed permission to wheel on roads, cross the borders, raise funds and give speeches, and every host country went out of the way to co-operate with him and welcome him.

In Rome, Pope John Paul II blessed the tour. In China, Rick was greeted by Vice Premier Wan Li who referred to him as a "hero of heroes." In London, England, he was escorted by the Queen's guards who closed London Bridge while Rick and crew posed for photographers. In New York City, Vancouver actor Michael J. Fox stopped filming when he heard Rick was in town and invited him to his studio to offer his support to the tour. In Poland, a policeman staged a mock arrest so an entire community could detain him for a homemade meal and a visit. And in the U.S.S.R., where he wasn't allowed to wheel (fear for his safety was given as the reason), Rick was permitted to talk to officials in rehabilitation centers and bring them his awareness campaign.

At every stop along the way Rick speaks about the three-part goal of his quest. First, he wants to create worldwide awareness of the potential of disabled people. He feels it's time to stop looking at people's disabilities and start looking at their abilities and potential. Second, he wants to raise money and generate an interest in wheelchair sports. He feels that a kid in a wheelchair won't take up sports or go on to succeed if no one has any expectations of him. Finally, his goal is to raise money for research in spinal cord injuries. Rick feels a lot of progress has been made in treatment of spinal cord injuries, but he's looking forward to the day that a wheelchair is something you see only in a museum. These are the reasons why Rick is pushing on.

Rick is still in motion as this story is being written–Christmas, 1986. This year Rick's Christmas will be spent in a hotel room in Northern Ontario with his five-man crew. Traveling with him are a physiotherapist, Amanda Reid, a psychologist, an advance man, a friend who doubles as a cook and person in charge of Rick's safety, and a friend who handles wheelchair maintenance. Without their vital assistance Rick could not have achieved his goal. Rick is not expected to reach Vancouver until June of 1987. However, Rick isn't thinking of that yet. He still has vast prairies to cross, winter storms to conquer and the Rocky Mountains to climb before he reaches home.

Up and down, up and down, 75 strokes a minute, 4,500 strokes an hour, 36,000 strokes a day, Rick Hansen, the wheelchair athlete and worldwide hero, is coming home.

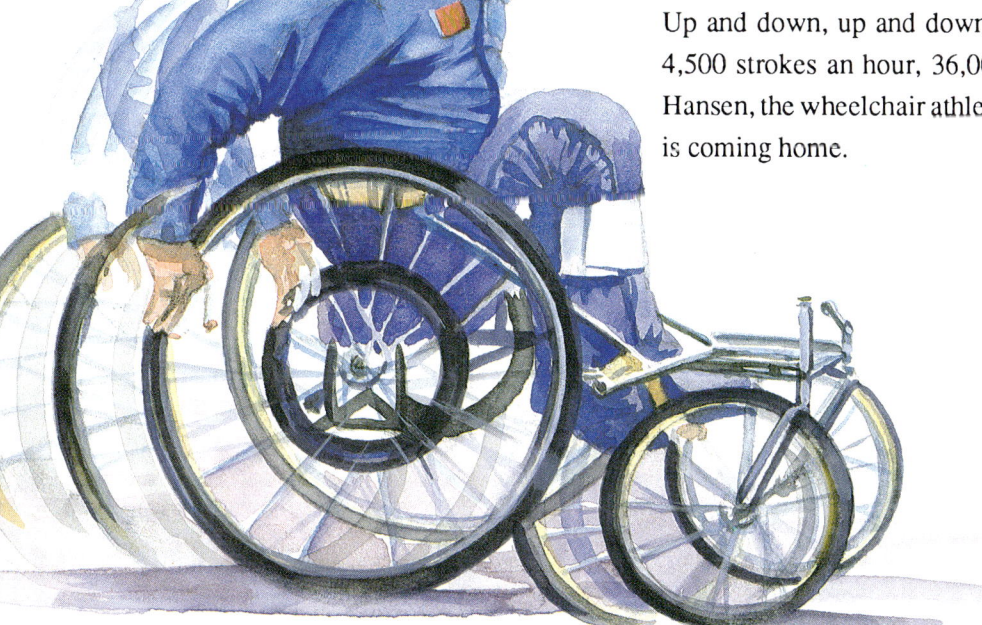

42

Ernest Hemingway

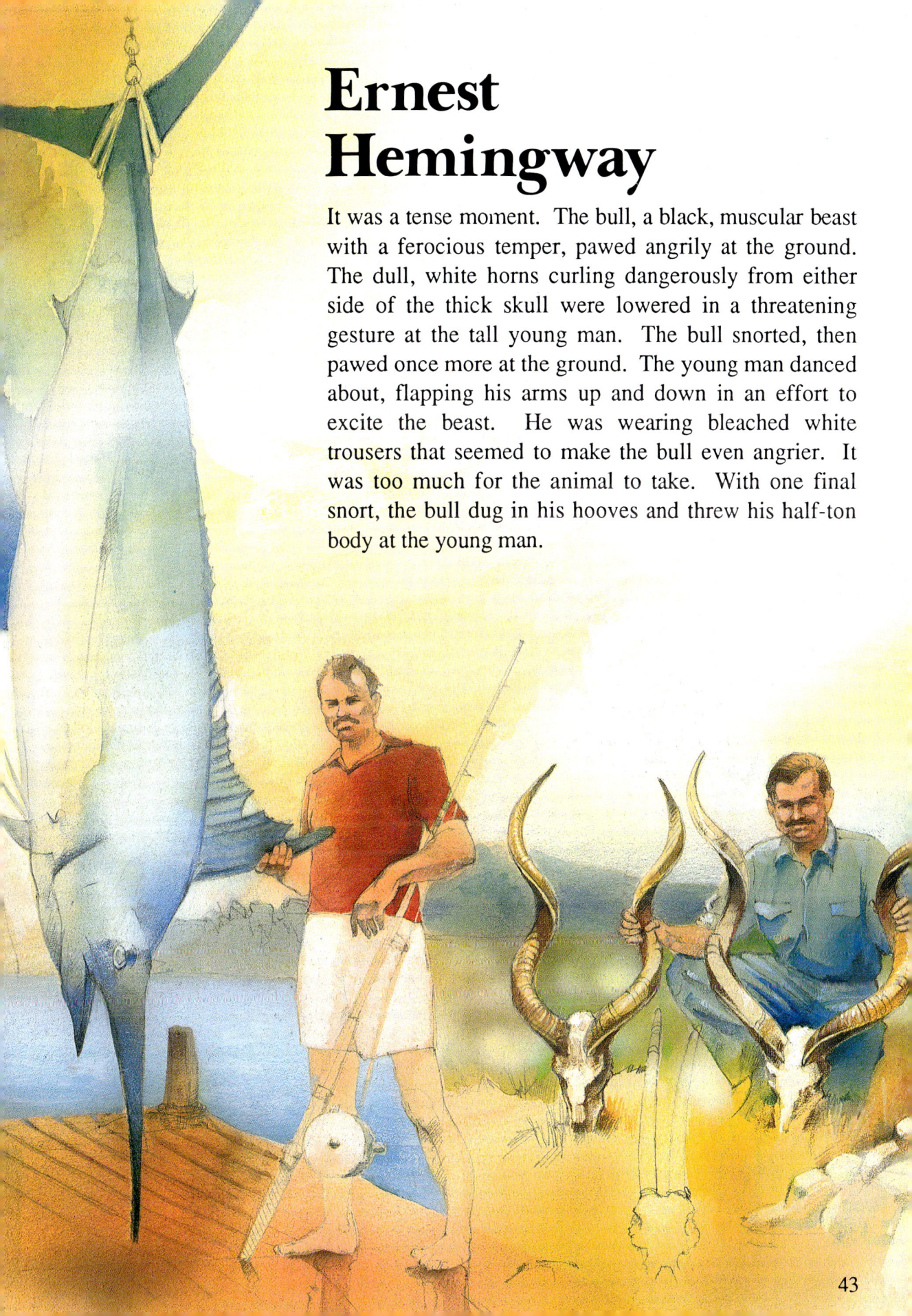

It was a tense moment. The bull, a black, muscular beast with a ferocious temper, pawed angrily at the ground. The dull, white horns curling dangerously from either side of the thick skull were lowered in a threatening gesture at the tall young man. The bull snorted, then pawed once more at the ground. The young man danced about, flapping his arms up and down in an effort to excite the beast. He was wearing bleached white trousers that seemed to make the bull even angrier. It was too much for the animal to take. With one final snort, the bull dug in his hooves and threw his half-ton body at the young man.

The man stood still, his limp arms hanging at his sides. The crowd grew quiet, watching and waiting for the fatal point of impact. The sharp tips of the bull's horns were aimed squarely at the man's chest. It seemed impossible that the young man could avoid the collision. The bull was less than ten feet away. It looked like the end for the foolish man in the white trousers. But the bull didn't kill the man. With only three feet to go, the young man stepped quickly to one side and laughed as the enraged beast charged past him. The thick shoulder of the bull grazed the young man's body, knocking him breathless to the ground. The crowd waited to see what would happen. The bull slid to a stop and looked from side to side, unable to understand what had happened. Another young man ran in front of the puzzled creature and began to flap his arms up and down. The bull forgot the young man laying helplessly in the dust as he sighted his horns on this new enemy. He snorted and pawed the ground. In another instant he was off and charging. The breathless young man in the white trousers got up slowly and brushed the dry, white Spanish dust from his clothing. He raised both arms in victory as the people on the side of the road cheered and whistled in salute to his bravery.

It was Pamplona, Spain, in the year 1924, and the young man had bravely endured the annual "run with the bulls." It was a special moment for the young man because he was also a famous writer who would one day immortalize this day in the sun in a novel. His name was Ernest Hemingway, a man who was to be regarded by many as the greatest American writer of the twentieth century.

Ernest Hemingway was born on July 21, 1899, in a large, comfortable home in Oak Park, Illinois. Oak Park, a suburb of Chicago, was nicknamed "Saint's Rest" because of the large number of retired clergymen who lived there. Ernest's father, Edward, was a family doctor who would rather have spent his life outdoors, pursuing the two sports he loved best -- hunting and fishing. During the summer holidays, Doctor Ed took his family to a cottage beside Walloon Lake on the shores of Lake Michigan where Ernest learned to love the outdoors. One of the first presents Ernest received from his father was a .22 caliber rifle that he learned to use with great skill. His father gave Ernest only one bullet a day. In this way he taught his son to respect the wildlife, while at the same time honing his sniper-like accuracy. In later years, Ernest would rely on his early shooting experiences at Walloon Lake as he journeyed on safari into the green hills of Africa.

Ernest saw action as an ambulance driver during World War I. He was wounded in Italy and later returned to Oak Park for recovery. Hemingway's famous novel *A Farewell to Arms* was based on his wartime experiences in Europe. Life in Saint's Rest now seemed boring to the young war veteran, prompting him to return to Europe as a news correspondent for *The Toronto Star*. While stationed in Paris, Hemingway made friends with a group of young writers and painters such as Pablo Picasso, James Joyce and F. Scott Fitzgerald.

One of the people responsible for shaping Hemingway's writing style was the American expatriote author, Gertrude Stein. Ernest spent many hours at Miss Stein's apartment at 27 rue de Fleurus in Paris, learning all he could about literature. Stein encouraged Ernest to submit his short stories for publication. Recognizing his genius as an author, she advised Ernest to avoid the use of fancy, complicated adverbs and adjectives, relying instead on simple, tough prose that in later years became Hemingway's trademark.

Ernest learned much about writing while living in Paris and later put his Parisian experiences into one of his last books, *A Moveable Feast.*

Hemingway loved Spain and often visited there with his wife and friends. He particularly liked the bullfights where the brave matadors battled "mano a mano" or hand to hand with the bulls. In his two books, *Death in the Afternoon* and *The Sun Also Rises,* Hemingway explored the drama of life and death in the bullring. In later years, during the cruelty and misery of the Spanish Civil War, Ernest Hemingway returned to Spain as a war correspondent, sending out detailed reports of the fighting between loyalist and rebel forces. Always at the center of any action, Ernest narrowly escaped death on several occasions, risking his life to get to the truth of a story. From his Spanish Civil War experiences, Ernest produced his next book, *For Whom The Bell Tolls.*

Ernest spent time in Africa, hunting lions, kudu, gazelle and waterbuck on the steaming hot Serengeti Plains of East Africa. Again, Hemingway used his first-hand experiences to produce a book, *The Green Hills of Africa,* as well as several excellent short stories including *The Snows of Kilimanjaro* and *The Short, Happy Life of Francis Macomber.*

By now, Ernest's fame was spreading throughout the world. He moved his family to Key West, Florida, where he immersed himself in yet another love -- deep-sea fishing. The warm Gulf Stream, flowing around the Caribbean and into the Atlantic, was rich in fish. Ernest went out daily, pulling in great catches of tarpon, tuna and marlin. In 1935, Ernest caught a mako shark that weighed 785 pounds, twelve pounds short of the world record. From his fishing experiences in Key West and later in Cuba, Ernest produced a novel that won him the Nobel Prize for literature, *The Old Man and The Sea.* He also used his Caribbean adventures in another book, *Islands in The Stream,* an account of an aging, lonely painter who finds meaning at the end of his life in a fight with Nazi submarines during World War II. In fact, Ernest enlisted in the United States Navy during World War II, serving as a submarine hunter off the coast of Cuba. He later saw action in Europe as a war correspondent, covering the major battles in Germany and France.

In all of his writings, Hemingway sought to explore the concept of suffering in human life. His heroes are usually solitary men who find little or no meaning in conventional society. Their integrity prevents them from conforming to the standards of others. Ultimately, the hero is beaten by the strength of the forces opposed to him. Although Hemingway's heroes were beaten, they were never destroyed, even if they were killed. To be destroyed, Hemingway said, a man has to consent to his own destruction. His heroes would never do that.

Toward the end of his life, Hemingway yearned for the quiet and solitude of the forest and the open sea. He made his final home in a large house on top of a hill in Ketchum, Idaho, where he died in 1961. In all he did, Hemingway sought to be as truthful to life as he could be. He used his own experiences as a hunter, deep-sea fisherman and bullfight fan in many of his books and short stories. His life was filled with excitement and action.

Although he spent many long hours working at his desk, Ernest Hemingway always took time to enjoy life. He proved, through his greatness as a writer, that life can be beautiful and exciting and that many of the common moments of a person's life are the most meaningful.

WAYNE GRETZKY

The score is tied 1-1 with two minutes left on the clock. It's been a tough game, but the crowd wants a winner. Hold onto your seat, folks, here he comes! Weaving, deking and carrying the puck, the young hockey player makes one last nifty head fake and flips it quickly into the net. The score -- Wayne Gretzky 2 -- Grandma Gretzky 1.

It's Saturday night on the farm in Canning, Ontario, twelve miles from the city of Brantford, Canada, and two-year-old Wayne Gretzky, destined to be known as hockey's "Great One," has scored another goal. His grandmother, Mary Gretzky, leans over in her big easy chair and rubs her shins. It's tough blocking goals against this future hockey champion, even at two years of age. She smiles, though. Grandma Gretzky knows that one day young Wayne will be a star.

Wayne Gretzky was born on January 26, 1961, in Brantford, Canada. Walter and Phyllis Gretzky, Wayne's parents, took the future National Hockey League star to his grandparents' farm every Saturday to watch *Hockey Night in Canada* on television. Wayne would imitate the players on TV, charging up and down the pine-planked living room floor, a pint-sized hockey stick in his hands, whacking away at a sponge ball. His grandmother was always the goalie.

From a very early age, Wayne's father encouraged his son to do his best. It wasn't enough to be average. If you had the talent, you had to use it. Wayne and his father would practice for hours on the 60' by 40' outdoor ice rink that Walter made each year at the back of their home. Walter would place old plastic bleach bottles on the ice as pylons for Wayne to skate around. He taught his son to control the puck and to anticipate changing situations. Walter strung light bulbs across the clothes line so that Wayne could practice his skating and stickhandling at night. Before long, the Gretzky ice rink became the most popular place in town, with local kids trundling over after school to play hockey with Wayne and his brothers.

Hockey wasn't the only sport that Wayne enjoyed as a youngster. A natural athlete, the lad adapted himself to the rigors of lacrosse, track and field and baseball. He became so skilled in baseball that years later the Toronto Blue Jays of the American League wanted Wayne to try out for a position on their team. Hockey always came first, and Wayne declined.

Wayne joined his first hockey team, the Nadrofsky Steelers of Brantford, in 1967. He was only six years old and playing against boys nine and ten years of age. In his first season he scored one goal. The next year he scored 27 goals, with 104 and 196 the two years after that. Then, in his final season with the Steelers (1971-72), Wayne knocked everyone over with an awesome 378 goals in 82 games!

It was during these formative years, as a minor league player, that Wayne began to feel the pressure of winning. He was such a natural goal scorer that his teammates and fans just expected him to win. Some of the fans weren't so kind in their treatment of the young scoring sensation. They booed and yelled at the youngster, forgetting that he was only a boy with easily bruised feelings. Wayne's father felt badly that his son had to endure such harsh treatment, but he encouraged Wayne to ignore it and to go out and do his best.

When Wayne was thirteen years old, he traveled to the Quebec City International Pee-Wee Hockey Tournament, the largest in North America. The papers ran front-page headlines of the young scoring whiz from Brantford. "Le Grand Gretzky," they called him. Fans flocked to the arena to get his autograph and to see him play. It was tough on the young player who was already being called the next Bobby Orr. Television, radio and newspaper crews followed him wherever he went. He was an instant sensation! His team made it to the semi-finals, but lost out to Oshawa 9-4. Wayne scored thirteen goals and thirteen assists in four games. The money raised in the tournament was used to help handicapped kids. Over 140,000 people visited the Quebec Colisee, 25,000 more than the previous year, to watch the scoring champion from Brantford play hockey.

Wayne went on to play for several teams in the years that followed, including the Junior A Sault Ste. Marie Greyhounds. He scored 70 goals and 112 assists in 64 games during the 1977-78 season with the Greyhounds. He was just sixteen years old. He won the league's Rookie of the Year and Most Sportsmanlike Player of the Year. The **Sault** Greyhounds gave Gretzky his famous number – 99. He wanted the number 9, in honor of his hero, Gordie Howe, but another player had it. Wayne picked the next closest number -- 99 -- and has worn it ever since.

At seventeen, Wayne turned pro with the Indianapolis Racers of the World Hockey Association. He finished the season with 110 points and was named WHA Rookie of the Year. One of Wayne's greatest thrills in hockey was playing on a line with his boyhood hero, Gordie Howe. The World Hockey Association All-Stars were to play a three-game series against Moscow Dynamo of the Soviet Union. The games took place at the Edmonton Coliseum in January, 1979. Gordie Howe had been Wayne's hero since the early days at the farm in Canning. Now Wayne had his chance to play with a hockey legend. Howe had just turned 50 and was a recent grandfather. His son, Mark, made up the third man on the Howe-Gretzky-Howe line. The trio were superb. Wayne scored his first goal of the series only 35 seconds after the opening face-off. The WHA All-Stars emerged as champions of the series, winning all three games against the team from Moscow.

In 1978, the WHA merged with the NHL, and Wayne was traded to the Edmonton Oilers, his present team. In his first year in the NHL, Wayne tied for the league scoring leadership with 137 points. He won the Hart Trophy (most valuable player) and the Lady Byng (most sportsmanlike player). In 1982, just before his 21st birthday, Wayne signed a 21-year contract worth over one million dollars a year. As a bonus, Oilers' owner, Peter Pocklington, gave Wayne his very own shopping center! It was all worth it. Wayne went on to lead the Oilers to two Stanley Cup championships, in 1984 and 1985.

Since 1978, Wayne Gretzky has broken practically every record in the NHL. His many awards include the Hart Trophy, the Art Ross Trophy (leading scorer, regular season), the Lady Byng, the Lester B. Pearson Trophy (NHL most valuable player as voted by other players), and the Emery Edge Trophy (player who appears in a minimum of 60 games and leads the NHL in plus-minus statistics). He was voted Sports Illustrated Sportsman of the Year in 1982, the Sporting News Man of the Year in 1981 and the Victor Award (excellence in sports in North America) from 1980 to 1984. In 1984, Wayne Gretzky became an Officer in the Order of Canada.

Through it all, number 99 has remained the decent, down-home person he has been since his boyhood days in the backyard rink in Brantford. Be the best you can be, his father always told him. Wayne Gretzky became the greatest!